My Dad's Alzheimer's

A Tribute

K. H. Tillquist

HART PRESS

Hart Press
Denver, CO
khtillquist@gmail.com

Printed in the United States of America

ISBN: 979-8-218-19937-1

Book and cover design: Sandra Jonas
Photographs: Hart family collection

Proceeds go to further Alzheimer's education and research in memory of Dale C. Hart.

*With love and appreciation to
my siblings,
Susan, Linda, Daniel, and David,
who are blessings in my life,
and to our children,
who shared life with our father,
their grandfather.*

*A special thanks to Neil
for his love and support.*

Author's Note

What follows is a poem describing the gradual and inescapable loss of my father to Alzheimer's. I have included photos from his childhood, World War II, and beyond, documenting the shared journey of our family. The poem is universal in its descriptions of the impact on those who bear witness to this devastating disease.

My father, Dale C. Hart, was raised in Boulder, Colorado. He attended Boulder High School and enlisted in the marines in May 1943, before turning eighteen. While serving in World War II, he earned four bronze stars in various battles in the Pacific theatre. When he returned to Colorado, he attended Denver University, becoming a teacher and then later an insurance agent. He raised five children in the Congress Park neighborhood, where he was active in the PTA and community and civic affairs.

Dad's passions included education for everyone. His goal when running for state senate in the 1970s was to increase literacy of all students and the graduation rate of Denver students, especially minorities. He also worked to support legislative and citizen efforts to maintain Denver's Capitol Hill area as a desirable place to live and work.

Among other things, he enjoyed spending time with his family and his dogs, reading, playing golf, and watching football. Diagnosed with Alzheimer's several years prior to his death, my father is remembered for his hearty laugh and generous spirit.

S. J. Webb
GROVE CITY, PA

There will be no remission
For him, there will be no cure
No joyous survivor,
Ribbon on his shirt

Catastrophic illness
ravages his mind
Photographs remain intact
The memory strip-mined

How cruel is this disease,
disassembling from within
Leaves not a trace of evidence
for the mirror or the skin

The laughter's still contagious
The grip remains as strong
Sixth-grade speech is effortless
Children's names often gone

Good mood ever present,
He works hard to engage
Rereads the funny papers
never turning the page

Visits warm with hugs and laughter
Tears help close the door
A brief update on current events
then stories about the War

Retired helmet on the shelf
Meant to protect and shield
Served young soldier, not grown man
To Alzheimer's did yield

Chance meeting at our bookstore
The warm, familiar place
I am his middle child
He did not know my face

Bittersweet melancholy
Travels from head to heart
How strange, how sad, to miss my dad
while sitting chairs apart.

Memories and stories
alive within my head
My daughters and I share them now
like sweet morsels of bread

Family portraits don't reveal
Mirrors cannot reflect
the slow, steady progression
of altered intellect

He has given timeless gifts
we are richer for receiving
Gifts reborn in daughters and sons
The legacy he is leaving

We're on a journey, slow and sure
where time becomes a thief
Courage is his passport
The currency, our grief

Oh! How I hate Alzheimer's
Our father is slowly dying
Perhaps these words are unshed tears
too bitter now for crying

Why place loss on paper now?
Find solace in believing
There is neither starting gun
nor deadline for the grieving.

The porch light of my father's soul
shines with a brilliant light
Why was this man chosen?
How can this be right?

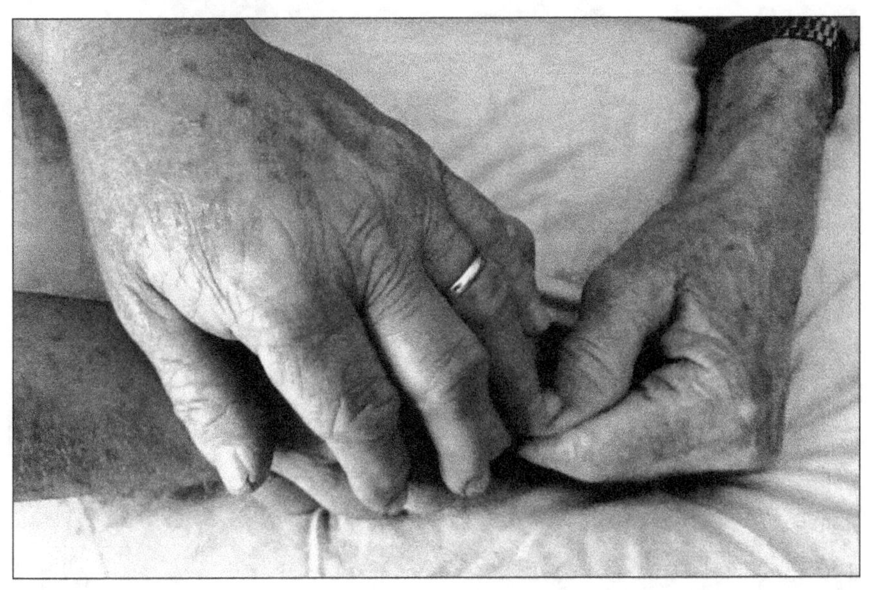

We watched him speak with Jesus
arms reaching, blue eyes wide
"Have I been a good boy, Lord?"
'Twas next morning that he died

Hand resting on his headstone
White marble cool to touch
I share all our stories
He doesn't say too much

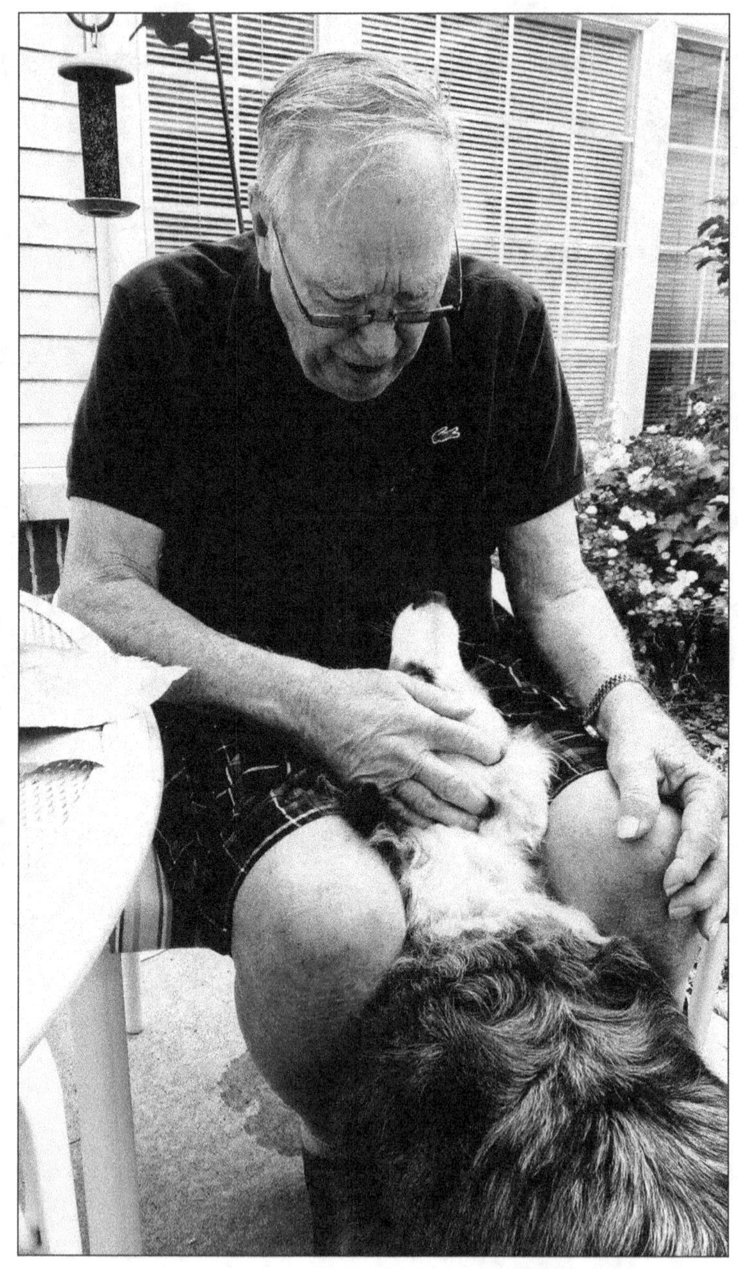

God bless this heart so giving
Not keeping track or score
Raised his family, lived life well
Deserving of much more

Christmas Prayer
by
Dale C. Hart

Our heavenly Father
We give thanks for the blessings
you have bestowed on us.

For the coming of Christ into our lives.
For children, relatives, friends.
For Santa Claus and the
bright Colorado sky.

We ask that you remind us
of the needs of others,
that we have much
while others have so little.

We ask aid for the many that are sick,
and hope for the oppressed
and depressed.

We ask that you provide us
the opportunity to serve
and be of use to others.

To all the world,
a joyous and peaceful New Year!

In Jesus's name,
amen.

My father wrote "Christmas Prayer" on the first Christmas following
the attacks on the World Trade Center in 2001.

I want to acknowledge friends who have also borne witness to this disease:

Celeste C, Ellen D, Judy Q, Cindy F, Mary N, Sheila C, Cheryl RC, Joani R, Gayle W, and Jill NF.

About the Author

Kerri Tillquist worked as a critical care nurse and nursing educator. She never intended to write a poem honoring her father and his battle with Alzheimer's. The verses came to her at night during his illness and following his death—a kind of healing process. Eventually, she had an entire poem. Proceeds from this small volume go to further Alzheimer's education and research in memory of Dale C. Hart. Kerri lives with her husband, Neil, in Denver, Colorado.